Contents

Highgrove

Highgrove is the private home of TRH The Prince of Wales and The Duchess of Cornwall, opened for others to share the enjoyment of their garden and to witness the successful organic methods used.

The Highgrove Shops offer a collection of organic foods and lifestyle products for the home and garden, all taking their inspiration from the garden at Highgrove. The majority of products have been created by British artisan manufacturers and craftsmen, reflecting the wide-ranging interests and passions of HRH The Prince of Wales.

'It is to achieve a sense of harmony that I have, over more than thirty years, worked with various people whose professional skills I admire in order to blend the arts of imagination and architecture into what, I hope, has gradually become a garden which delights the eye, warms the heart and feeds the soul.'

HRH THE PRINCE OF WALES – HIGHGROVE

History of Highgrove

It is now more than thirty years since the Duchy of Cornwall bought Highgrove in Gloucestershire and HRH The Prince of Wales made the Estate his home.

Originally styled 'High Grove', the house was built between 1796 and 1798 in a Georgian neo-classical design on the site of an older property; the most likely architect was a local mason, Anthony Keck. Immediately prior to His Royal Highness's arrival, Highgrove was the home of Maurice Macmillan whose father, Harold Macmillan, was the British Prime Minister in the late Nineteen-Fifties and early Sixties.

Since 1980, both the house and garden have been the subject of many thoughtful and innovative changes. When the Prince first arrived, Highgrove possessed little more than a neglected kitchen garden, an overgrown copse, some pastureland and a few hollow oaks.

Today, after the hard work of scores of people, the garden unfolds in a series of highly personal and inspiring tableaux, each one reflecting the Prince's interests and enthusiasms.

Highgrove is also the location of Home Farm, part of the Duchy of Cornwall, which has developed into a centre of excellence for organic farming and gardening, as well as an acknowledged haven for wildlife.

Above all, Highgrove is the family home of Their Royal Highnesses The Prince of Wales and The Duchess of Cornwall.

Orchard Room and Orchard

The Orchard Room was built in 1998 to accommodate the many meetings HRH The Prince of Wales hosts at Highgrove for his various charities and organizations. It was built in a Cotswold style to fit in with the farm buildings and has stone pillars similar to the Market House in Tetbury.

Outside are four teak chairs beneath the loggia which were designed by Leon Krier (the architect and master-planner of Poundbury), and the limed oak bench was a fiftieth birthday present to the Prince from the Duchy of Cornwall. The two small arbours opposite the loggia were designed by Charles Morris for the Highgrove Garden which was exhibited at the 1998 Chelsea Flower Show. The inscriptions inside are taken from the works of William Blake.

The Orchard of old heritage varieties of apples given by the Brogdale Horticultural Trust in Kent includes *Malus*, 'Hunts Duke of Gloucester', 'White Junety' and 'Devon Buckland', and is under-planted with the low catmint *Nepeta x faassenii* and *Muscari* 'Early Giant'. It also contains one specimen tree, a Glastonbury Thorn, which flowers at Christmas time. The tree was a gift from the Abbot of Glastonbury and is a descendant of the original thorn, which, according to legend, was brought to England by Joseph of Arimathea when he visited these shores with the young Christ.

Shand Gate

The Shand Gate, a Highgrove stone and oak gate house with reclaimed 18th-century Indian doors from Jodhpur, forms the entrance to the Cottage Garden. The gate is named in memory of the Duchess of Cornwall's late brother Mark Shand. Gifts from India hang inside.

Cottage Garden

Through the Shand Gate is the Cottage Garden which is divided into two parts, old and new.

The new Cottage Garden is planted with a yellow, pink and blue theme, reflecting the colours of vibrant Tibetan silks using a mix of herbaceous plants, bulbs and shrubs. The trees include a Holm oak, a Princeton Gold maple, a black mulberry and variegated tulip trees. Busts in the yew hedge are of Maurice Macmillan and Alan McGlashan.

In contrast the old Cottage Garden, designed originally by the Prince and the late Rosemary Verey, features a typical English planting scheme: a mixture of trees, shrubs and herbaceous plants, with spring and autumn flowering bulbs, intended to provide year-round colour. An oak summer house designed by the Prince and Mark Hoare was built here in 2013 by the Highgrove estate team using local oak.

A circular stone seat of Derbyshire gritstone, designed by Julian and Isabel Bannerman and made by masons from Hereford Cathedral, encircles a topiarized English yew.

Nearby is a bust by Frances Baruch of Sir Laurens van der Post, a close friend of the Prince.

Mediterranean Garden and Rose Pergola

The Box Topiary Garden was redesigned as the Mediterranean Garden in 2010 due to box blight, a disease which decimates *Buxus* as a species. This garden now contains rosemary, lavender, hebes, salvias and cistus.

Overlooking the garden is Cecilia Maxwell-Scott's bronze bust of Leon Krier.

The 'T' shaped Rose Pergola was a fiftieth birthday present to the Prince and designed by Charles Morris. Climbing roses, wisteria, clematis and honeysuckle are planted here.

Built into the wall above a stone seat is a sculpture in French limestone of Laocoön, the Trojan high priest. The original is in the Vatican Museum in Rome, and this impressive copy was made from memory by Albanian sculptor Andrian Melka.

The topiary, five spheres and five cubes of English yew, are being clipped to represent the five Platonic and first five Archimedean solids which are fundamental architectural building blocks.

Oak Pavilion

The 60ft cedar (over two hundred years old) died much to the despair of the Prince and was consequently partly felled during the winter of 2007. It was 'an organic counterweight to the Georgian architecture of the house'. On its site, an open oak pavilion topped by a spire has been constructed, designed by the architect Mark Hoare, who studied at the Prince's Foundation for Building Community.

Adjacent is a semi-circular seat made by Stephen Florence from Somerset Ham stone, Highgrove oak and wrought iron. The seat faces the acid bed, which was created to grow a collection of azaleas, rhododendrons and specimen magnolias given to the Prince by Edmund de Rothschild from his Exbury Gardens in Hampshire.

Thyme Walk

An avenue of clipped golden yew, the only remnant of
the original garden, lines the Thyme Walk. At the Prince's
suggestion, these yews were clipped into eccentric geometric
shapes and beneath them a mixed aggregate path is inter-
planted with more than twenty different varieties of thyme,
and now golden marjoram and primroses. A hornbeam stilt
hedge encloses the Walk on two sides. Around the main lawn
there is a striking topiary yew hedge, designed by Sir Roy
Strong, which takes on average six weeks to trim.

Terrace

The Terrace was one of the first gardens created at Highgrove and the result of a combination of Lady Salisbury's and the Prince's designs. It contains plants chosen and planted entirely by His Royal Highness. The stonework on the Terrace and walls was created by Fred Ind, who has been working at Highgrove for over thirty years.

The low fountain at the Terrace's centre, which flows over a millstone, was designed by the Prince and sculptor William Pye. The pepper-pot pavilions, placed at the two corners, were designed by the Prince. Quatrefoil windows echoing those of the pavilions have been cut into the yew hedges beyond.

The tiles inside the pavilions were designed by the Prince and crafted by architect Christopher Alexander in order to reflect the Mexican orange blossom that grows here.

In 2010 four large olive trees were planted on the Terrace: they are approximately 150 years old and have come from Spain. Great care has to be taken in winter to protect these trees as they are not used to our cold and wet winters.

Sundial Garden

Lady Salisbury originally designed the Sundial Garden as a rose garden with soft herbaceous planting. Now the garden features a bolder colour scheme of blues, pinks and purples, with delphiniums being the focal plant. This colour scheme now runs through the garden. The architectural bones of this garden remain the same with the beds edged with box hedging and old olive oil pots. Scented climbers include jasmine, *Rosa* 'Highgrove', clematis, and a blue and white wisteria. The high yew hedges are clipped with windows which hold four busts of the Prince at various stages of his life; these were gifts from the sculptors.

Willow structures are also used in the Sundial Garden; these have been created from willow harvested from the reed sewage bed. In summer they provide support for plants and act as focal points in winter.

The sundial, from which this garden takes its name, was a present from the late Duke of Beaufort and outside gardeners and staff, while the wrought-iron gates were found in a reclamation yard and restyled by Julian and Isabel Bannerman, and topped with The Prince of Wales's feathers.

Highgrove Façade

From the front of the house it is possible to catch a fine view of St Mary's, Tetbury's Gothic Revival-style parish church, which is situated about a mile away across parkland. Between 1890 and 1893, William Yatman, a previous owner of Highgrove, paid for the rebuilding of the church's spire so that he and his successors could continue to enjoy such a splendid view.

The gentle curve of the front drive is lined with lime trees. In summer, various wildflowers including ox-eye daisies, knapweeds, scabious and Common Spotted Orchid appear on both sides of the drive.

The house has been improved with the help of artist Felix Kelly: a rather stark stone parapet was replaced with an urn-topped balustrade, and a pediment and Ionic pilasters were added.

The original informal plantings of shrubs and climbers have grown well to further soften the façade of the house. To the right is a free-form box hedge which is referred to as the cloud hedge.

Running North-East across Tanner's Park towards Longfurlong Lane, a half-mile avenue of some sixty-six red twig lime trees leads the eye to a tall cast-iron column. Once part of London's Victoria Station, it was saved from demolition and topped with a metal 'stork and nest' sculpture designed by Julian and Isabel Bannerman.

Wildflower Meadow

Stretching from the front drive to the back drive, the ever-changing Wildflower Meadow covers about four acres of ground. Miriam Rothschild developed the original seed mixture with thirty-two species in 1982. Seed-rich green hay is brought in from Clattinger Farm, South Cerney, to introduce more species year-on-year. It is managed as a traditional hay meadow, cut in July/August for hay or silage by scythe and harvester.

From September to December the meadow is grazed closely by sheep to move the seed around and open the sward for fresh seed to germinate. Yellow rattle is used to keep the grasses down and now over five different types of orchids are found. This is now the Coronation Meadow for Gloucestershire.

Trees include a mix of oaks, sweet chestnuts, horse chestnuts, balsam poplars and a National Collection of beech. Naturalised daffodils include the Lent lily and 'Ice Follies'.

A fastigiate hornbeam avenue divides the meadow and links the ornamental gardens around the house to the Kitchen Garden. This is under-planted with *Camassia*, *Fritillaria meleagris*, *Gladiolus byzantinus* and *Tulipa sylvestris*. At the end of the avenue is a 'ribbon of red' created with plantings of Japanese maples and copper beech which colour well in the autumn.

Azalea Walk

The Prince wanted this walk to be special and chose to place busts of people whom he admires on one wall: Sir John Taverner, the musician/composer; Dame Miriam Rothschild, wildflower expert/insectologist; Patrick Holden, former Director of the Soil Association; Doctor Vandana Shiva, an Indian environmental campaigner; The Rt Revd and Rt Hon. Richard Chartres, The Bishop of London; Doctor Kathleen Raine, poet and scholar; and The Dowager Duchess of Devonshire. Further along the wall is a bust of Lord Mountbatten and one of HRH The Prince of Wales.

At the southern end of the walk is a statue of Diana, The Goddess of Hunting.

The Azalea Walk contains azaleas in large Italian terracotta pots, under-planted with hardy ferns and spring flowering *Chionodoxa sardensis*. The Bath stone doorway carved by students from the Prince's Foundation for Building Community includes a mouse and a bird's nest, designed to represent Highgrove's relationship with nature. The inscription in Egyptian hieroglyphics over the doorway translates as: 'The flowers in the garden are a reflection of the stars in the sky'.

To the left of the doorway is a memorial to Tigga, the Prince's much-loved Jack Russell Terrier who died in 2004 and is buried here. The carving is by Marcus Cornish.

Kitchen Garden

At the time when the Prince moved to Highgrove this area of the garden was virtually derelict. With the help of Lady Salisbury, he set about planning a patriotic kitchen garden of one acre in size.

New areas for growing were marked out with box (*Buxus sempervirens*) hedges in the shape of the crosses of Saint George and Saint Andrew. These create eight discrete triangles and eight squares, which provide most of the vegetable needs of the house. The vegetables are entirely organic and meet the high standards of the Soil Association, of which the Prince is Patron. Due to box blight the box hedges were removed in 2008 and replaced with *Teucrium x lucidrys* (germander).

There are a mix of fruit trees planted in the Kitchen Garden along with some ornamental plantings, espalier and free standing. A mixed apple tunnel runs through the garden under-planted with hellebores and primulas. In the centre is an Italian fountain sourced for the garden by Lady Salisbury with a carp pool around it. A herb garden surrounds it.

There are central herbaceous borders with Highgrove's colour scheme of pinks, blues, purples and whites, and sweet pea and runner bean tunnels.

Adorning a quiet corner is a bronze wall plaque of the Green Man, by the sculptor Nicholas Dimbleby, inscribed 'Genius Loci' (Spirit of a Place).

Arboretum and Sanctuary

Many rare and ornamental trees have been planted to include magnolias, flowering cherries, crab-apples, Katsura, beech, Judas trees, and Japanese maples. Azaleas, rhododendrons, viburnums, cornus, hydrangeas and daphnes are also found here: the combination of these trees and shrubs gives all-year-round interest and a spectacular autumn colour display. *Narcissi* 'Thalia', 'Sun Disc' and 'Hawara', scillas, cyclamen, winter aconites, snowdrops and puschkinia are planted under the trees.

Within the Arboretum is a bronze, presented to the Prince by the late American sculptor Frederick Hart, titled 'The Daughters of Odessa: Martyrs of Modernism' and dedicated to all oppressed people of the world. The sculpture is partially surrounded by a curved oak seat with Carmarthenshire stone.

The Sanctuary was built in 1999 to mark the Millennium and is a place of contemplation. Based upon the principles of sacred geometry, it was devised by Professor Keith Critchlow of The Prince's School of Traditional Arts and created from a design by Charles Morris. It is made entirely of natural materials, with cob (earth) walls, Bath stone footings and pillars, and a Cotswold stone roof. A lintel over the oak door is inscribed with the evening collect 'Lighten our darkness we beseech thee O Lord'.

Winterbourne Garden

Originally an abandoned area outside the Kitchen Garden, the planting was initially started in 1999. It was suggested that this sheltered site might offer protection to tender plants found in the southern hemisphere. A number of tree ferns, presented to the Prince by the British Pteridological Society of which he is Patron, were planted.

The cold winters of 2010 and 2011 caused unfortunate losses. Replanting has been done with panicled hydrangeas, *Philadelphus*, flowering *Cornus*, *Ceanothus*, and mahonia for colour, scent and longevity of display.

The set of attractive double gates of green oak with bronze fittings were designed by Charles Morris and made by Stephen Florence.

The stone bench in this area was given to the Prince by the Saints and Sinners Club of London.

A winterbourne stream runs through this area and is planted with *Gunnera* and Asiatic *Primula*. The stream is bounded by a stone wall which is supported by three arched 'buttresses'.

Stumpery

The Stumpery was initially created by Julian and Isabel Bannerman and is based on a Victorian concept of growing ferns amongst tree stumps. The majority are sweet chestnut and oak. At its heart are two classical temples built from green oak which have been cut to resemble stone, with pieces of tree root decorating the pediments. At the base of a tall oak sits David Wynne's sculpture of a wood nymph, the Goddess of the Wood.

The thatched tree house, formally known as 'Hollyrood House', was designed by William Bertram in 1988. It was originally in a holly tree which died but now stands upon a rustic platform of oak, made by Stephen Florence, supported by shards of Welsh slate and Carmarthenshire limestone steps.

Nearby is the Japanese Moss Garden, which was created as a gift from Iue International and the Highgrove Florilegium Japanese Team. A replica of the Isis (based on the Egyptian Ibis) features in the Moss Garden.

In 2002 the Stumpery was enlarged to house a new National Collection of large and broad-leaved hostas – one of the Prince's favourite plants.

At the southern edge of the Stumpery, the 'Wall of Gifts' contains various pieces of architectural stone, some of

which were given to the Prince, while others have been collected by him. There are also pieces made by students from the Prince's Foundation for Building Community.

The Temple of Worthies, created by the Bannermans from green oak, has been drilled and sandblasted to give the impression of being 'rusticated' stone. In the centre is a bronze relief of Queen Elizabeth The Queen Mother sculpted by Marcus Cornish.

The Stumpery's water feature reuses redundant stone which has been mixed with holey limestone and crowned with a canopy of *Gunnera*, Chilean or Giant Rhubarb.

Lily Pool Garden, Laurel Tunnel and Buttress Garden

At the end of the Thyme Walk is the Lily Pool Garden. Enjoying all-day sun, this garden was planted in a Mediterranean style with large terracotta jars placed in each corner.

Further on from the Lily Pool Garden stands a bronze of the Borghese Gladiator, a copy of the one at Houghton Hall in Norfolk and a present to the Prince from its owner, Lord Cholmondeley.

Leading on from the Thyme Walk is a lime avenue with a dovecote at its end, a gift from the Sultan of Oman.

The Laurel Tunnel, with its cobbled path, houses a fern collection and a stone seat made from 'architectural rescue' pieces designed by Julian and Isabel Bannerman. At the centre of the tunnel is a stone obelisk.

The Buttress Garden is enhanced by two pillars of redundant ecclesiastical stone topped with braziers. Relatively new yew hedges have been clipped into steps which butt up against the old yew hedge forming compartments. These areas are planted with distinct colour schemes.

Carpet Garden

HRH The Prince of Wales took inspiration for this garden from a Turkish carpet at Highgrove House. He wanted to translate the geometric shapes and colours in the carpet into a living garden. With the help of others to bring the design to fruition, the resultant garden won a Silver Medal at the 2001 Chelsea Flower Show.

The Carpet Garden was transferred to Highgrove where it was enclosed by completely new walls, much like ancient urban gardens in the Middle East.

Its Eastern style is echoed by the ceramics placed by the plantings. The garden is filled with scented roses, both climbing and shrub forms, clematis, sweet peas (*Lathyrus cupani* and *Lathyrus sativus* var. *azureus*), asters, salvias and peonies. Climbing roses include 'Sander's White' and 'Highgrove'.

The walls are lined with Italian cypresses, a favourite of the Prince. The Carpet Garden also contains olive trees, cork oaks and vines.

Organic Sustainability

Highgrove has been organic since the Prince arrived; the aim is that the Gardens should be in complete harmony with nature. Ethically sound management policies are pursued based around a closed system designed to maintain fertility within the Gardens by recycling all waste materials. For example, wood chip is used for fuelling the biomass wood-burning stove, as well as being used as plant mulch; leaf mould is a substitute for peat and compost; and compost 'tea' replaces plant food/fertilizer and plant conditioners. All rainwater is collected to be used for irrigation, and solar panels, ground source and air source heat pumps are used for heating.

A specially built reed bed sewage system is used for all Highgrove's waste water and all vegetable food waste goes through the composting system.

The garden is as self-sufficient as possible with minimal seed or potting compost bought in. Biological pest control, rather than pesticides, is used to combat pests.

Renewable and sustainable energy systems are used on the Estate wherever possible. Highgrove is living proof that organic methods can work to the benefit of both man and nature.